Original title:
The Pear's Path

Copyright © 2025 Creative Arts Management OÜ
All rights reserved.

Author: Adrian Caldwell
ISBN HARDBACK: 978-1-80586-342-7
ISBN PAPERBACK: 978-1-80586-814-9

Rising with the Morning Dew

A fruit so round and bright,
It dances in the light.
With laughter in the breeze,
It tickles all the trees.

The sun comes up to play,
While squirrels shout hooray!
They chase it up and down,
A jolly, fruity crown.

Old bees start to hum tunes,
As lazy cats watch moons.
The grass is fresh and green,
What a funny scene!

With every laughing round,
They bounce upon the ground.
A jig of joy unfolds,
In dew drops, fun beholds!

Dancing with the Wind

In breezy fields, the giggles soar,
While leaves do dance and spirits roar.
A twist, a turn, all nature prances,
Even the grass takes funny chances.

A squirrel flips, it cracks a grin,
Chasing shadows, let the fun begin!
With every gust, a tickling tease,
Nature laughs with perfect ease.

Sylvan Secrets

In hidden nooks where secrets creep,
The trees share tales while owls peep.
A rabbit hops, with mischief bright,
Steals a glance, then bolts in fright.

The brook chuckles, it can't contain,
As frogs leap high—oh, such disdain!
With every splash, a joke is told,
Nature's laughter, brave and bold.

Nature's Winding Ways

A winding path where daisies glide,
With each step, the giggles hide.
A ladybug rolls, a clumsy stunt,
On petals soft, it takes the front.

The sun peeks in, a cheeky grin,
As butterflies dance, they spin and spin.
Their fluttering wings hum silly songs,
Nature's giggles where joy belongs.

Echoes of the Orchard

In orchards lush, a chorus sings,
While apples tumble like bowling rings.
The laughter echoes, a playful shout,
As bees buzz loud, there's no doubt.

A cat stalks low, all stealthy and sly,
But slips on grass, oh my, oh my!
With every crash and little squeak,
Nature's humor sets the week.

Blooms and Fragrance Forgotten

In a garden where gnats dare play,
The blossoms giggle throughout the day.
Sneaky bees plot with a goofy grin,
As flowers stumble, their dance begins.

A crown of petals perched on a bee,
Laughing at flies who buzz with glee.
Colors collide, a comical crew,
In this bustling world, a fragrant zoo.

Unraveling the Essence of Eden

With a wink, the fruit whispers secrets untold,
An apple's snicker, a peach's bold,
Under the tree where mischief takes flight,
They chortle and sway, a hilarious sight.

The garden is ripe with a chuckling breeze,
Fruit rolling over, causing a tease.
In the shadow of laughter, they gather and play,
Unraveling joy in a quirky ballet.

Riding the Winds of Canopy

High on branches where the squirrels zoom,
The leaves throw parties, creating a boom.
Dancing on air, they twist and shout,
Inviting all critters to join the rout.

A parrot croons, adding to the fun,
While the raccoons clap 'till the day is done.
As acorns tumble, the giggles grow loud,
Riding high waves, the trees are proud.

Bursting with Life's Juices

Drenched in sunlight, the fruit laughs out,
Juicy and jolly, that's what it's about.
With each bite taken, the flavors collide,
A comedy show where taste buds slide.

In sticky sweetness, the humor will flow,
Fruits juggle flavors in a row.
Bursting with joy, they hold up a cheer,
Life's juicy story—bring on the jeers!

The Orchard's Embrace

In a grove where laughter grows,
Fruits nibble on silly toes.
Bouncing balls of juicy glee,
Nature's jesters, wild and free.

Squirrels wear their hats askew,
Chasing shadows just for you.
Sunlight winks from leafy heights,
Tickling cheeks with golden sights.

Beneath the Leafy Canopy

Under branches, whispers dance,
Caterpillars in a trance.
With every giggle, fruits unite,
Creating banter, pure delight.

Bees in bowties buzz along,
Humming to a silly song.
Leaves clap hands in gentle mirth,
A world of joy, a merry birth.

Nature's Silent Course

In twilight's hush, the pranks unfold,
Apples laugh, their stories bold.
Lemons juggle in the breeze,
While cherries tease the bumblebees.

Underneath a sky so vast,
Bananas dream of races past.
With every twist and every grin,
Nature's jesters break the din.

Fruits of Reflection

Pineapples wear their crowns with pride,
While plums play hide and seek inside.
Each fruit a jester, bright and round,
In this lively, merry ground.

Grapes giggle, twirling tight,
As oranges joke in pure delight.
In this harvest of surprise,
The orchard sings, it never lies.

A Tree's Gentle Tread

In the orchard, trees do sway,
With their roots, they like to play.
Wobbling round as leaves take flight,
Hiding squirrels that peek in fright.

Barking dogs and buzzing bees
Join the dance with rustling leaves.
When the sun begins to shine,
Branches tickle, oh so fine!

Harvest Dreams

Pies are baking, oh what glee!
Dreams of sweetness, come with me.
Gather round, the laughter's grand,
Fruits of labor in our hand.

Carts are rolling, wheels do squeak,
Jokes are shared, and smiles peak.
Juicy stories start to flow,
As we munch on treats we grow.

Ripening in the Sun

Swinging softly as we grin,
Life gets fruity with a spin.
Tickled by the golden rays,
Days grow sweet in so many ways.

Chasing shadows, catching light,
Bouncing cheeks, oh what a sight!
Nature's giggles fill the air,
We all dance without a care.

Branches of Fate

Whimsical winds whirl around,
Tickling branches, ticking sounds.
Fortune swings on leafy vines,
Mischief thrives where sunlight shines.

Frisky breezes twist and bend,
Every branch, a quirky friend.
Fulfilling tales of laughter bright,
In this orchard, pure delight.

Woven in Nature's Melody

A fruit in a tree with a grin so wide,
Giggling at bees as they pass on by.
Leaves whisper jokes in the summer heat,
While squirrels engage in a dance so sweet.

The wind tells tales of a juicy plight,
As branches sway gently, a comical sight.
A fumble, a tumble, oh what a cheer,
Nature's own circus, laughter's premiere.

Unfolding in Nature's Canvas

Brush strokes of green on a bright sunny day,
Colors collide in a whimsical way.
Chubby little fruits hang, plump and round,
They tickle each other when no one's around.

A painter's dilemma with sticky sweet hue,
Crisp laughter echoes, no one knows who.
The canvas alive, with mischief it beams,
As fruits dream in colors of giggly dreams.

Dance of the Ripened Fruits

In the orchard's ball, everyone is spry,
Fruits twirl and whirl 'neath a giggling sky.
A pear in a tutu, a peach in a tie,
Join in the fun as they bounce and fly.

The rhythm of ripeness brings joy unconfined,
With chuckles of nectar, sweetness entwined.
They shimmy and shake, no worries, just glee,
Each moment a jest in this fruity jubilee.

Through the Lattice of Time

A lattice of laughter, woven with care,
Where time strolls slowly, without a single scare.
The fruits exchange secrets with the passing breeze,
While the sun winks boldly, and whispers with ease.

Seasons play tricks, a funny charade,
As squirrels steal kisses, and plans are made.
Through laughter and ripening, all in the scheme,
The boundless joys weave a whimsical dream.

The Unwritten Stories of Harvest

In orchards full of golden gems,
The squirrels dance like cheeky friends.
With every pluck, a giggle springs,
As laughter flies on autumn wings.

A farmer trips, his hat takes flight,
The pumpkins giggle in delight.
The apples roll with merry cheer,
Sneaking bites when no one's near.

The baskets overflow, but too many pears,
They start a riot, beyond repairs.
They juggle fruits, what a sight to see,
An unplanned show of pure jubilee.

And when the sun begins to dip,
The harvest moons do a silly flip.
With every laugh, a story's told,
In harvest's heart, where joy unfolds.

A Palette of Autumn Hues

In trees of crimson and golden glow,
The leaves put on a dance-like show.
A jaunty breeze sweeps through the air,
As nature prances, without a care.

The pumpkins wear a goofy grin,
While acorns rustle, teasing kin.
The corn stalks wobble, just like they've sprouted,
With every step, giggles are spouted.

The wind paints skies in strokes of glee,
While the birds hum songs of harmony.
A cheeky crow steals one last bite,
As evening falls, the stars ignite.

Beneath the branches, shadows play,
Creating scenes of silly ballet.
Each color sings, a joyful muse,
In autumn's show, we can't refuse.

Rhythms of Nature's Delight

In fields where sun and laughter blend,
The grasshoppers hop, what a legend!
They chirp their tunes, a jolly beat,
As daisies sway on happy feet.

Bees buzz along, in a silly race,
Chasing dreams at a frantic pace.
They bumble and stumble, what a scene,
Nature's circus, so vivid and keen.

The river giggles as it flows,
Tickling rocks in a comical pose.
Frogs leap high with a bulging grin,
Embracing the chaos where fun begins.

From warm light of dawn to dusk's sweet song,
Nature invites us to tag along.
With every beat, a chuckle near,
In this wild dance, we share the cheer!

Under the Watchful Sky

Beneath a dome of cloud and blue,
The sun winks down with a playful hue.
While shadows stretch and tickle toes,
A magic spell of fun bestows.

The wind whispers tales of faraway lands,
As children chase with giddy hands.
Kites soar high, twisting through air,
While giggles echo without a care.

The squirrels gossip with acorn plots,
While gathering snacks in big, silly knots.
One cheeky critter steals a snack,
As friends join in with a playful whack.

When stars emerge in the twilight's grace,
The world settles down in a sleepy embrace.
But dreams of laughter drift high and free,
Under the sky, we all just "be."

Boughs of Serenity

In a tree so high, a fruit did sway,
It wobbled and giggled, come out to play.
With a bounce and a jiggle, it danced in the air,
Singing to bees, with not a single care.

'What's the buzz?' asked a cheeky old crow,
'Just hanging around, don't you know?
Life is just sweet, like the sunlight so grand,
I'm a fruity philosopher, a true fruit stand!'

The Blooming Horizon

A blossom woke up, bright yellow and round,
Dreaming of places where laughter is found.
'Let's roll with the wind!' the petals declared,
While squirrels nearby whispered, 'Oh how they dared!'

Chasing the clouds with a skip and a twist,
Each giggle and grin, no fruit could resist.
They tumbled and turned, in the warm sunny glow,
Creating a circus, as friends came to show!

Reflections in Ripening Fruit

A mirror of green, a reflection of fun,
The flavor of laughter, bright under the sun.
Each fruit had a tale, with giggles to share,
As they swapped all their stories without a care.

"Once I had legs!" said a plump little fig,
"Did a jig in the breeze, oh I felt so big!
But my dance card was full, I tripped on my stem,
Now I lounge in the sun, a sweet jelly gem!"

Journey to the Sun-kissed Core

Off on a trip to the land of delight,
Nuts, fruits, and berries, oh what a sight!
With a pit-stop for laughs at the fountain of juice,
A splash here and there, they felt so recluse.

'Let's get squished!' cried the grape, with zesty intent,
'Juice flows like laughter!' they all were content.
Underneath the bright sky, they danced in a swirl,
As each fruity giggle unfurled in a twirl!

Embracing the Sunlit Trail

Beneath the bright and shining rays,
Fruits dance along in merry plays.
A squirrel twirls, his acorn hat,
While birds sing songs of chatty chat.

Rolling down on golden grass,
Giggling leaves in breezes pass.
A pickle vine throws jokes at pears,
As everyone just laughs and stares.

The sunlight paints a silly scene,
Where rhymes and riddles intertwine keen.
With every step, the chuckles spread,
As nature's jesters frolic ahead.

So grab a snack, maybe a roll,
And let this garden tease your soul.
With fruit and fun in every way,
We cheerfully embrace the day.

Whims of the Wind-swept Grove

In a grove where giggles bloom,
The breeze bursts in with cheeky zoom.
A dandelion tickles the nose,
While a pear plays hide and seek in rows.

The wind wears a crown of wild flowers,
Prancing about for silly hours.
With whispers of mischief floating near,
The trees chuckle, filled with cheer.

A rabbit juggles tiny seeds,
While bouncing along, ignoring needs.
And every leaf shares a playful wink,
As laughter bubbles up like a drink.

So join the frolic, don't delay,
Let joy and folly have their way.
In this grove, with nonsense at its core,
We find the fun, and then some more.

Harvest of Dreams

In fields where giggles grow like grain,
We gather smiles, forget the rain.
With baskets wide, we catch some fun,
As sleepy fruits bask in the sun.

A cabbage rolls, with great delight,
Claiming it's a pear, oh what a sight!
While pumpkins dance and carrots tease,
The grains hum softly in the breeze.

With every harvest, laughter flows,
As silly faces strike funny poses.
A chorus of giggles fills the air,
With friendship sprouting everywhere.

So fill your basket with glee today,
As we munch on apples on our way.
This nonsense feast makes our hearts beam,
In this joyous, tasty dream!

Orchard Whispers

In orchards rich with tales and sights,
The laughter swells like fruity heights.
A grape slips by, a cheeky jest,
As friends assemble for a quest.

With every step, a chuckle found,
As fruit hangs low, the jokes abound.
An apple wears a funny grin,
While peaches swirl in a dance of spin.

The whispers play upon the vine,
As nature leans in, "Hey, it's fine!"
Each tree a storyteller fair,
With tales of nonsense everywhere.

So join the fun beneath the leaves,
Where humor grows and joy retrieves.
In this orchard, let's not hurry,
To savor jokes and endless flurry.

The Lush Road Ahead

Beneath the trees, we prance and play,
With laughter loud, we greet the day.
A fruit so round, it hides in greens,
It winks at us, like silly teens.

A stroll with friends, in sunlit glee,
We chase the wind, unshackled, free.
Through dreams and giggles, we navigate,
On this lush road, we celebrate!

Oh, berries bop, and apples sway,
While we trip over roots, in disarray.
"Hey, look a frog!" a voice will cheer,
As we skid and slip, our joy sincere.

With every turn, a new surprise,
A world where everything's made of pies.
In fruity realms, we find our bliss,
This road ahead, we shall not miss!

Unraveled Roots

Tangled vines and roots that tease,
Trip us up, oh what a breeze!
We laugh and tumble, roll and sigh,
In this garden, time flutters by.

A twisty path leads us around,
Where gnarled branches play the clown.
"Watch your step!" a friend will shout,
As we tumble down, laughter about.

Beneath the boughs, we trade our tales,
Of silly shoes and whimsical fails.
Each root a story, each laugh a gift,
In this maze of mirth, we find our lift.

With feet all tangled, we dance anew,
In this orchard, we're never blue.
For every stumble adds to the cheer,
In the realm of fruits, there's nothing to fear!

The Serpent of Ripeness

A twisty thing, with skin so smooth,
It weaves through branches, ready to groove.
A sneaky fruit, with cunning flair,
In this garden, we're caught unaware!

"Is it ripe?!" a voice will croon,
As we squint up at the glowing moon.
With frantic dances, we search the trees,
For treasures hidden—"Look, it's a tease!"

Its curves invite a cheeky grin,
For every bite feels like a win.
We pinch and poke, in playful jest,
This serpent of ripeness knows us best!

Eager giggles fill the air,
As we chase sweetness with silly flair.
With every taste, we color our day,
In this funny orchard, we laugh and play!

Sweetness in the Breeze

In the warm air, the flavors tease,
While sugar dances on a soft breeze.
Fruits parade in hues so bright,
Each plump surprise brings pure delight.

A whiff of fun, a splash of cheer,
As we spin 'round without a fear.
Giggling echoes, through trees they race,
In this fruity world, we find our place.

Sticky fingers, laughter's song,
We munch and laugh, nothing feels wrong.
A taste of joy, a splashy bite,
This sweetness in the breeze feels right!

So let's frolic, my jolly friends,
As the fruit fest never ends.
With every crunch, we stake our claim,
In this jesting garden, we're all the same!

Tales of Sweetened Breezes

Beneath the boughs the laughter flows,
With fruity tales where mischief grows.
A squirrel danced with a funny flair,
And stole my snack without a care.

The bees are buzzing, let's all cheer,
They've got a party, come grab a beer!
With honey hats and nectar cups,
Watch out for ants, they'll steal your ups!

One pear winks, it's quite a tease,
It plops right down, oh what a breeze!
The giggles rise as fruit takes flight,
Who knew the orchard could delight?

So let us sing of juicy pranks,
And frolic where the sweet juice ranks.
These tales we tell, they never fade,
In breezes sweet, our laughs parade.

The Hidden Treasures of Orchards

In gardens lush, the secrets glow,
With buried gems where wild things grow.
A gnome with shades and a cheeky grin,
Hides shiny treats, let the fun begin!

Amidst the branches, wild tales ensue,
A band of fruits sing a tune or two.
With vines that twist and apples that roll,
The orchard's stage has quite a soul.

One fruit tries a daring leap,
To join a dance, but it falls with a beep!
The laughter bursts, it's all in jest,
In hidden treasures, we find our best.

So gather round, the fun's our guide,
With each sweet moment, our hearts abide.
The orchard whispers with joyful nears,
A treasure trove of life and cheers.

Essence of Flora's Embrace

In blossoms bright, the jokes unfold,
Where petals sway and stories told.
A daisy mocks, "I'm all alone!"
While twirling with a stinky cone.

The tulip's wink, it's quite a sight,
It teases bees, then takes flight.
With fluttering dreams and scents to share,
The garden's fun is beyond compare!

"Oh look, a bumble!" cries a rose,
"Who said romance isn't full of woes?"
With peonies giggling in full bloom,
They laugh away the scent of gloom.

In flora's dance, we find our cheer,
A fragrant laugh, a friend so dear.
Join in the joy that nature brings,
In this embrace, our laughter sings.

Footprints on Fertile Ground

Each step we take, a tale erodes,
In fertile fields, where laughter bodes.
A duck in boots makes quite a scene,
It struts around, a clumsy queen!

The footprints of fun scatter wide,
As creatures gather, they all abide.
A rabbit hops with a cheerful grin,
While folks just wonder what's held within.

A dance of hooves, a wiggle or two,
What magic brews just out of view?
In every scar on this trusty ground,
Are secrets rich, where joy is found.

So stroll along, leave laughter there,
Footprints marked with spark and flair.
In nature's realm, our hearts collide,
With funny tales, we take a ride.

From Blossom to Bounty

In spring the blossoms giggle high,
They wave their petals, oh so spry.
A bee comes buzzing with a grin,
"I'll make you sweet, let's begin!"

As summer warms the lazy breeze,
The branches sway, as if to tease.
"Look at me, I'm growing round!"
The fruit is laughing, joy unbound.

When autumn comes, with harvest cheer,
The fruits all dance and shout, "We're here!"
In pies and jams, we find delight,
From tiny buds to tasty bites!

The Golden Orchard's Saga

In an orchard where the sunbeams play,
A fruity tale begins today.
Gold and green in a jolly throng,
Chortling leaves in a merry song.

The branches sway like party-goers,
Finding joy in refreshment pourers.
"Pick me first!" the apples tease,
While pears just giggle in the breeze.

With each new fruit, a story grows,
Of daring dreams and funny foes.
They flaunt their hue, with playful grins,
In this grand orchard, laughter wins.

Taste of the Earth

A plump delight hangs oh so low,
"Come take a bite!" the fruit does crow.
With juicy tales that make you grin,
Each taste reveals a sweet, new spin.

The ground beneath starts tickling toes,
As roots wiggle like silly shows.
"We're here to bring some laughter too!"
The earth smells fresh, a vibrant brew.

When wind whispers through the leaves,
It carries giggles, sheer reprieves.
From orchard's heart to mouth, we race,
In every bite, a joyful trace!

Spreading Seeds of Adventure

Little seeds in a playful flight,
Whisper, "Let's explore that height!"
With every toss, they giggle loud,
"We'll make our home beneath a cloud!"

The winds declare, "Let's take a ride!"
As laughter dances, wild and wide.
A journey starts with roots so bold,
Each seed a story waiting to unfold.

Through valleys deep and hills we peek,
Their dreams and schemes are far from meek.
From soil to sun, a wacky quest,
Seeds spread smiles, it's simply the best!

Nectar in the Gloaming

In twilight's gleam, a fruit takes flight,
With juicy dreams that dance in sight.
It rolls with glee, no care at all,
On winding paths, it makes a call.

The bee in jest, a bumbling fool,
Attempts to sip from golden pool.
But slips and spins, with buzzing cheer,
And falls right in, oh my, oh dear!

A garden scene, where laughter flows,
With friendly bugs, and worn-out toes.
They share a tale of silly woe,
As fruit and critters steal the show.

So raise a glass to nectar sweet,
Where giggles sprout from every treat.
In gloaming light, we laugh and play,
Embracing joy, come what may.

The Weight of Burdened Limbs

Oh branches heavy, what a sight,
With fruits that wobble, side to right.
They hang like stars on a seesaw swing,
While squirrels below, in chaos, cling.

A gust of wind, a fruit takes flight,
It sails right past that hungry kite.
A plop, a splat, a comedic mess,
As laughter breaks the stillness, yes!

The branches creak, they start to bend,
With every munch, we need a friend.
Come join the feast, it's quite a show,
As weights of laughter make limbs glow.

In nature's grip, where fun abounds,
Among the leaves, hilarity sounds.
From burdened limbs, we find our cheer,
With every smile that draws us near.

Solace in Swaying Silhouettes

In shadows cast from trees above,
A dance unfolds, a tale of love.
The fruits sway softly, side to side,
In giggles shared, they seem to glide.

A fox tiptoes, oh what a sight,
In pursuit of snacks, with all its might.
But trips on roots, and blunders down,
With laughter echoing all around.

The moon peeks in, a curious face,
As critters gather in merry chase.
With fruits among the charming play,
The night unfolds, in bright array.

Swaying silhouettes, a soothing sight,
In nature's humor, pure delight.
We laugh and sway beneath the trees,
As joy takes wing upon the breeze.

Where Blossoms Whisper

In gardens lush, the blossoms speak,
Of fruity dreams, both bold and cheek.
They giggle soft on breezy nights,
With hints of mischief, pure delights.

A beetle winks, a friendly face,
As petals sway in gentle grace.
It tugs a stem, with all its power,
To bounce around like springtime flowers.

Each whisper shared, an inside joke,
With fruits and blooms that gently poke.
They swap sweet tales of sunny days,
As laughter intertwines in playful ways.

So find your joy where blossoms play,
In every rustle, sip, and sway.
With nature's charm, we laugh and cheer,
For in this garden, fun is near.

Chasing Evening Shadows

In the garden where I roam,
A lazy cat claims my home.
I trip on roots, I tumble down,
While squirrels laugh, that cheeky crowd.

The sun dips low, my feet are slow,
I dance with shadows, go with the flow.
With every leap, I hear them squeak,
Those twirling trees, they play hide and seek.

The grass gets plush, the breeze is light,
I'm the jester, what a sight!
In this twilight, life's a game,
My silly slips ignite the flame.

So here I stand, a gleeful fool,
In evening's glow, I'm breaking the rule.
With each mishap, I giggle more,
At nature's laughter, I soar and explore.

Serenity at the Root of It All

Beneath the tree, I find my glee,
With roots that wriggle like a bumblebee.
I sit and munch on an apple free,
As branches sway like they too agree.

A wind gust blows, my hair's a mess,
I chuckle loud, I must confess.
The birds above begin their show,
Synchronized in nature's glow.

The ants parade in lines so neat,
As I watch closely, they skip a beat.
With every wiggle, they dance, oh dear,
I laugh aloud, they can't quite steer!

So here I sit, a peaceful sight,
Among the roots, beneath the light.
Life's little quirks taste sweet, not wrong,
In this whimsical world, I belong.

Over the Hills of Green and Gold

I saunter forth with a clumsy grin,
Past hills of green where my tumble begins.
A goat looks up, and to my surprise,
He bleats a joke; he's wise in disguise.

The daisies giggle as I pass by,
I swear they wink with a fluttering sigh.
A butterfly flutters, it stalls in the air,
As if to whisper, "Do you even care?"

Rolling down slopes, I'm free like a bird,
Each tumble and flip is absurd and blurred.
With nature laughing, I join in the spree,
A riot of joy, a feast of glee!

At dusk I find, with my humor intact,
The hills I roamed, a place to relax.
With skies painted gold, I bid the day,
In this dance of folly, I'll forever stay.

Tranquil Footsteps in the Dew

In early morn, when the world is still,
I stumble through dew on a playful hill.
Each step a splash, a sparkling spree,
With grass all soggy, but oh, so free!

The sun peeks shyly, a sleepy yawn,
While I pirouette on the brightening lawn.
Dewdrops swerve in a wobbly line,
As if nature said, "You're doing just fine!"

Around me bloom the flowers, bold,
With irony wrapped in petals of gold.
A bee buzzes loudly, it's quite a show,
And I can't help but dance toe to toe!

When laughter rings out from bushes nearby,
I'm drawn to the humor under the sky.
In each joyful footstep, let the fun brew,
For life's but a game in the morning dew.

Sun-kissed Sanctuary

In a garden so lush, oh so bright,
A fruit rolled away, what a sight!
It danced down the hill, quite a spree,
Yelling, 'Catch me, I'm free as can be!'

A squirrel chased it, all in a blur,
While a snail sat back, ready to stir.
He shouted, 'Slow down, take your time!'
As the pear scooted off, plotting a rhyme!

A bird in a tree tweeted a tune,
'You fancy a dinner? Join me at noon!'
With a waddle and spin, that pear made its move,
Spilling juice everywhere, oh what a groove!

The flowers all laughed at the pear's silly jig,
As bees buzzed around, doing a jig.
The sun winked down on this wondrous show,
A sanctuary of giggles, watch it glow!

Beneath Blue Canopies

Underneath stretches of heaven so bright,
A pear rolled on grass, what a sight!
It tumbled and giggled, soft and round,
While crickets applauded, leaping around.

A worm peered out, wide-eyed with glee,
'Can you dance with us, oh fruit so free?'
The pear just chuckled, spun on its stem,
Joining the dance, a rogue little gem!

A breeze carried jokes, the leaves took a bow,
As the pear boogied under the high bough.
It slipped on a puddle, yelping in fun,
'This is my ball, oh, look at me run!'

Sunbeams were laughing, as shadows would weave,
While critters grew tired, ready to leave.
But the pear was just starting, its joy in full bloom,
Spinning through laughter, a flower in gloom!

An Epiphany in the Orchard

In an orchard of dreams, a light bulb went off,
A pear thought aloud, with a giggle and scoff.
'Why not roll far, see the world on a spree?
Adventure awaits, come dance along with me!'

With a bounce and a wiggle, it started to roam,
Past bushes, past twigs, it felt right at home.
Bumbles of laughter echoed in its trail,
As friends joined in, each telling a tale.

A bee, with a buzz, couldn't resist,
Joined the fun, said, 'Now that's on my list!'
They danced through the blooms, like stars in a race,
That giggly green fruit was leading the pace!

With every new turn, fresh laughter would flow,
Even the sun had to stop for the show.
In that wild orchard, the merriment grew,
Round and round they'd go, sharing laughter anew!

Gifts of the Gathering Storm

As clouds rolled in with a fuzzy gray hue,
A pear peeked out, 'What's this we'll do?'
It wobbled with glee, preparing for fun,
Saying, 'I'm the gift, come join, my dear ones!'

Raindrops began tapping, a dance in the air,
With a splat and a plop, it spun without care.
The puddles erupted in splashes galore,
As laughter broke free, from each leafy decor.

A goat on the hill thought he'd take a chance,
Joined the pear rolling, in a slippery dance.
Together they chirped, through the thunder and rain,
With each silly slip, they conquered the plain!

And when the sun peeked to end all the fun,
A rainbow stretched out, the world had just spun.
That pear grinned wide, its party begun,
In the gifts of the storm, oh, what a run!

Ripples in the Orchard's Mirror

In the orchard, fruits with glee,
Chasing shadows, sipping tea.
A squirrel scolds in grand parade,
While blossoms giggle, unafraid.

The trees sway, their fruit a show,
Great ideas born from the low.
Chubby cheeks and laughter bright,
As we dance beneath the light.

Wobbling ducks in pink ballet,
Stomp their feet, come what may!
A bumblebee plays the drums,
Jam sessions for all who hum!

Laughter mingles with the breeze,
Orchard fun, a sweet tease!
As twilight twirls its golden skirt,
We share stories, squishy and hurt.

An Interlude of Life and Light

Underneath the old oak tree,
Chasing dreams, so wild and free.
A raccoon dons a fancy hat,
While the rooster sings, 'How about that?'

Butterflies in a haphazard race,
Trip on petals, oh what a face!
Laughter spills like spilled milkshake,
Sweetness flows, make no mistake.

Admiring clouds, what do we see?
A rabbit dressed in stripes—whoopee!
He jumps high, the crowd goes wild,
This silly show, oh how we're styled!

Fireflies join the evening play,
Flickering like stars on display.
The night wraps us in a cozy hug,
Where joy is brewed in every mug.

Harvesting Moonlit Wishes

Beneath the moon, we gather round,
Whispers of dreams and laughter sound.
Jars of joy lined up in rows,
Harvesting wishes, who really knows?

A fox in boots, he struts with flair,
Claiming the orchard as his lair.
With a grin that seems to glow,
'Tonight we feast,' he says, all aglow!

The night sky dances in delight,
As pumpkins giggle, holding tight.
With every wish, a story spins,
Bathtubs full of moonlight wins!

Chasing shadows, we swirl around,
In nature's arms, we all are found.
Under stars, with hearts so bold,
Together we share the tales untold.

In the Embrace of Nature's Bounty

Grinning apples, a crunchy crew,
Holding court with berries too.
Cherries argue about their hue,
While a stoic pear says, 'I'm true!'

The sun pops up, a jolly face,
Dancing rays all over the place.
Even squirrels can't hold their cheer,
They toss about, ''Tis the year!'

Bananas in a line, they slide,
With laughter echoing far and wide.
A grape-tastic jamboree, they cheer,
Rolling smiles, come grab a sphere!

In leafy lanes, we chase delight,
Fruitful frolics under starlight.
In nature's clutch, we grasp our fate,
Celebrating here, it feels so great!

Embracing the Tang of Life

A fruit with a grin, so round and tight,
Bouncing through gardens, what a sight!
Scaring the bees with its playful prance,
Who knew a pear could lead a dance?

Chasing the breeze, it rolls away,
Hiding from squirrels, oh what a play!
Under the sun, it twirls and spins,
Laughing at life, where the fun begins.

With juicy laughter, it teases the tree,
"Catch me if you can!" Oh, wild and free!
Sipping on sunshine, it giggles, oh dear,
Sprouting wisecracks with every cheer.

In this orchard of joy, where silliness reigns,
A pear's crazy antics weave laughter's chains.
Life's sweet but sour, a wobbly glee,
Join in the fun, let's all be carefree!

Blossoms on the Wind

Petals and laughter dance in the air,
While fruity companions embrace the flair.
A piquant giggle, a reminder to sing,
Join in the revelry that nature brings!

Through blossoms that bounce, a festival flows,
Where mischief abounds, anything goes!
As blooms share a wink with the fruit in a race,
Chasing each other in this grand embrace.

In this bouquet of bliss, there's cheer all around,
With bees buzzing jokes, and bees buzzing sound.
The laughter of flowers, bright and sweet,
Turns every moment into a treat.

So let's sway with the breeze, let our spirits take flight,
As blossoms ignite our hearts with delight.
With every soft whisper, let happiness bloom,
For life is a garden—we're here to consume!

The Spirit of Verdant Realms

A jolly green vine gives a wink from the gate,
Chasing the sun, with a twist of fate.
Leaves rustle secrets of giggles untold,
Where nature's sweet humor never grows old.

A cucumber chuckles, a squash tries to grin,
While tomatoes gasp, with a cheeky spin.
In the heart of the patch, laughter sprouts wide,
Bouncing around on a whimsy tide.

A party of roots, dancing with flair,
Wiggling together, the soil is their lair.
With each silly tumble, they banter and tease,
In this verdant realm, it's a laugh with ease.

So let's tiptoe softly, in harmony sway,
To the jokes of the greens, come join the display!
With mirth in the earth, we grow hand in hand,
In gardens of giggles, we all understand!

A Tapestry of Flora and Light

Threads of green weave through the bright,
A tapestry blooms, oh what a sight!
With daisies that chuckle and dandelions tease,
Nature's grand canvas aims to please.

Each stem a story, each leaf a joke,
With blossoms that giggle, the wonders provoke!
They play in the daisies, they dive in the sun,
In this field of laughter, all are welcome, come run!

The colors are vibrant, like laughter on air,
As petals confide, "You're welcome to share!"
So tie up your shoes, take a hop or a skip,
Join in the dance, let your worries slip!

A spectacle of life, with humor so grand,
In nature's bouquet, we together stand.
With smiles and bright hearts, we weave day and night,
In this tapestry woven of flora and light!

Glistening Trails of Flora

In the garden, bright and fair,
A little critter, unaware.
Danced through blooms with quite a flair,
Stumbled once, found mud to share.

Petals whispered, laughed in glee,
"Watch your step, come dance with me!"
Wiggly worms held back their snickers,
As bees buzzed 'round, without their flickers.

A ladybug spun in delight,
Chasing sunbeams, oh what a sight!
Frogs croaked tales of silly nights,
Under moonbeams, shining lights.

Thus in laughter, blooms do sway,
Nature's joy in bright display.
With every leaf, a joke to share,
In the garden, love is rare.

The Melody of Nature's Heart

Squirrels play their nutty tunes,
While the flowers dance in prunes.
Crickets keep the lively beat,
As daisies tap their tiny feet.

Breezes blow with chuckling sighs,
Tickling leaves, those perfect spies.
A butterfly played peek-a-boo,
While flowers giggled, "What's the view?"

Underneath the shady trees,
Birds shared gossip on the breeze.
"Did you see the cat last night?
Dressed in shadows, such a fright!"

Harmony in every glade,
Nature's music never fades.
With laughter in every part,
Playful tunes, a work of art.

A Symphony of Orchard Tales

In an orchard, mischief brews,
Apples swapped out for old shoes.
Cider barrels roll with glee,
While laughter rings from every tree.

A raccoon played a game of hide,
In peachy dust, he chose to slide.
"Catch me if you can!" he cried,
While the pears rolled, filled with pride.

Cherries blushed in cheeks so red,
As pears joked, "We wish we led!"
"Let's form a band," they chirped with zest,
"Together we will be the best!"

Underneath the starlit sky,
The fruits sang tunes and let out a sigh.
Joy in every ripe affair,
In this orchard, none compare!

In Pursuit of Nature's Symphony

Down the trail, all creatures roam,
Searching for their leafy home.
Laughter echoes, paws in flight,
Chasing shadows in the light.

A raccoon's hat is quite the show,
Cuckoo birds say, "Oh, let it go!"
Afraid of mud, the fox slips twice,
While crickets roll in great delight.

Sunflowers nod with sunny chats,
While a hedgehog wears the hats.
"Let's form a parade!" they cheer so loud,
Beneath the whimsy, nature's crowd.

With every wiggle, shimmy, shake,
A song of silly dreams they make.
Life's a dance, a joyous spree,
In this concert, we are free!

Golden Curves of Destiny

In the orchard where the laughter flows,
Golden fruits wear their sunny clothes.
They wiggle and wobble, quite a sight,
Dancing with joy in the warm daylight.

Bouncing around like little suns,
Playing tag, oh, what fun runs!
A squirrel joins in with a cheeky grin,
Claiming he's king, let the games begin!

The branches groove with a joyful swing,
As ants do their merry little fling.
Each bite divine, a burst of glee,
Life's sweetest moments, oh where's the key?

So grab a friend, or two, or three,
Enjoy the show, it's comedy!
With golden curves, oh so round,
In this orchard, pure joy is found.

Sweetness Amongst Thorns

In the garden where mischief thrives,
Sweet treats pop up, oh what great dives!
Thorns may prick, but laughter's strong,
Who knew life could be this fun and wrong?

With jackets of green and stabs of red,
These fruits giggle from their leafy bed.
They play hide-and-seek, oh so sly,
Underneath the watchful sky.

Wandering pests, with nimble toes,
Try to leap to where the sweetness flows.
Yet every step is a wild dance,
As they twirl and yell, "Give me a chance!"

So here's to sweetness caught in thorns,
A circus of joy where the fun adorns.
In this funny garden, take a stance,
For sweetness is here, come join the dance!

Traces of a Ripened Soul

In a world where happiness is high,
Ripened gems droop low, oh my!
Chasing sunshine with silly grace,
Each bounce forward, an eager race.

A fruit pranks a passing bee,
"Buzz off buddy, you can't have me!"
With giggle-filled juice, it's hard to hold,
As laughter spills in shades of gold.

They sway in fun, and have their say,
Under the moonlight, come what may.
Each chuckle echoes through the leaves,
Life's little joys, what one believes!

So mark the trail of sweetness bold,
With traces of giggles, and stories told.
In ripened souls, the jesters play,
In orchards vast, come join the fray!

In the Glistening Green

Amidst the glistening hues of green,
Life plays out like a comic scene.
Fruits toss jokes from the boughs up high,
"Take a bite, but I might fly!"

In the crunch of laughter, we find our way,
As berries banter and sway all day.
They tease the birds with a fruity plea,
"Sing a song, and fly with me!"

The sun dips low, painting stories bright,
With giggle-wrapped dreams in soft twilight.
Each shimmer dances, tickling the air,
As fruits play tag without a care.

So gather round, let the laughter glean,
In this orchard, tranquil and keen.
With glistening green, joy is seen,
Every moment cherished, truly serene!

Journey of Juicy Secrets

In a garden so lush, a tale unfolds,
Where whispers of fruit and giggles are told.
A pear in disguise, oh what a sight!
Hiding from ants, trying to take flight.

With friends like the apple, so round and so bright,
They jest about life, oh what pure delight!
"I'm sweet enough," a ripe pear exclaims,
While others send jabs, like fruit-themed games.

Every breeze has a story, a chuckle, a sigh,
As they roll in the sun, feeling oh-so spry.
Join their escapades, laugh till you weep,
In this fruity world, secrets run deep.

So next time you munch on a juicy treat,
Remember their journey, oh isn't it sweet?
A playful romp through orchard's embrace,
Where sweetness and laughter always interlace.

Tangy Echoes Beneath Leaves

Under the branches, a chatter arises,
With juice-soaked secrets and messy surprises.
A pear takes a tumble, lands with a thud,
Laughing so hard, it creates a small flood.

"Watch out, here comes the squirrel on a spree!"
Cried the brave fruit, oh so full of glee.
With a bounce and a jiggle, the pear runs away,
While nuts fly about like in a wild ballet.

The vine's tangled whispers, so full of cheer,
Fruits poke and tease, 'It's your turn, my dear!'
Each moment a cackle, a prank, or a jest,
In the canopy's shade, they giggle the best.

When shadows get long, and laughter does fade,
The fruits gather round, sharing jokes they've made.
With sweetness and tang, they savor the fun,
Echoes of laughter until day is done.

A Fruitful Odyssey

Upon a branch high, a pear daydreams,
Wishing to join the world of wild schemes.
With whimsy as armor, it leaps for a ride,
Down to the ground, in excitement, it slides.

"The world is so big, I must taste every flavor!"
Said the cheeky pear, quite the fruity savior.
With a twist and a turn, it rolls down the hill,
Finding new adventures, its heart full and still.

Then came a carrot, who danced with delight,
"Come join me, dear pear, the party's tonight!"
With laughter and music, both sweet and absurd,
They twirled in the moonlight, without a word.

As the journey unfolds with each mischievous plan,
They'd visit the garden—an odd little clan.
With smiles and silliness, together they'll roam,
In a land filled with joy, forever their home.

Shadows of Sunlit Boughs

When sunlight spills gold on the orchard's green,
A gathering of fruits, all curious and keen.
The pear tells a tale of a daring escape,
From a kitchen so daunting, it had to reshape.

"Oh the knife was so sharp and the forks were all mean!"
Cried the pear in a joy that was truly serene.
With friends all around, they roared with laughter,
Imagining ways to outrun disaster.

The orange chimed in, "Let's form a parade!
We'll flaunt our fine peels, we won't be afraid!"
So they wobbled and jigged, the shadows did dance,
In delightful confusion, they seized every chance.

As dusk whispered secrets to each lively leaf,
They celebrated moments, beyond all belief.
In shadows of boughs where the soft breezes sigh,
The fruits find their joy, as the moon climbs the sky.

Seeds of Wanderlust

In a garden where seeds take flight,
A globular fruit dreams of the night.
Twisting and turning, a slippery quest,
Bouncing along, it's never at rest.

With companions like bugs and a snail,
They chat about life in the glimmering trail.
"Why not roll down this hill oh so steep?"
The pear grinned wide, "I fancy a leap!"

They tumble and laugh in the golden light,
Chasing their dreams, what a comical sight!
Planting their feet on the whims of the breeze,
And poking fun at their friends with great ease.

But as the sun sets with a wink and a grin,
They find themselves smothered in soft, leafy skin.
With a giggle they call out, "What a lovely mess!
Wanderlust? More like a juicy success!"

Juiced Journeys in Twilight

A fruity adventure under stars that gleam,
Where citrus scents twirl in a hazy dream.
A pear grandly boasts, "Ready for flight!
I'm juiced up and ready for fun tonight!"

On a vine swing they bounce to and fro,
"I can't believe the places I'll go!
From high tree tops to muddy ground,
I'll slip and slide, but never be found!"

With each wobble and giggle through the cool dusk,
They crack silly jokes, fueling each husk.
"We're ripe for adventure, come spin with the breeze,
Let's make merry mischief, just squeeze if you please!"

As the moon peeks out to join in their fun,
All glows with laughter, the party's begun.
In twilight's embrace, their journey avowed,
Juiced journeys are best among the loud crowd!

Beneath Boughs of Green Gold

Beneath old boughs where the shadows dance,
A pear plans plots with a mischievous glance.
"Let's prank the apples, they think they're so sweet!
We'll roll on the grass, can't wait for the feat!"

A chorus of giggles from all in the shade,
"The best kind of laughter is never delayed!"
So off they all tumble, a bouncy brigade,
Hatching their schemes in the fun that they made.

But as they go rolling, a little confused,
They find that their plans are somewhat abused.
For weary old limbs and too much fruit juice,
Cause hiccups and giggles, and chaos ensues!

Yet under the boughs, a tale to be told,
Of friendships and fun, plus tales that unfold.
So here's to the laughter, all ages embraced,
Beneath lovely branches, with grandeur and haste!

Life in the Shade of Abundance

In a shady nook where the joy overflowing,
Fruits gather 'round for the fun that is glowing.
A pear with a grin, its charm a delight,
Says, "Grab your pals, it's a party tonight!"

With laughter and games, they roll here and there,
Playing tag 'til their sides ache from flair.
A playful debate flares, who's the best friend?
"Us pears are the best, in the fun we transcend!"

"What about mango," a voice chimes with glee,
"It's ripe for the picking, just wait and you'll see."
But the pear starts to huff, what a comical scene,
"Juicy debates, how silly, I mean!"

As night draws near, stars begin to twinkle,
With a soft soothing sigh, they all start to crinkle.
In abundance they rest, sharing stories so bright,
Life with your friends is a beautiful sight!

Through Gnarled Branches

In a twisty tree with a silly grin,
A fruit decided to spin and spin.
"Catch me if you can!" it cheered with glee,
As squirrels danced around, as quick as can be.

The branches creaked, the leaves would shake,
While a hungry deer eyed the sweet mistake.
But the fruit was clever, it played the fool,
"I'm not just a snack, I'm the star of the school!"

A raccoon laughed, with paws held high,
"It's not every day you see grapes that fly!"
They giggled and wiggled, all under the sun,
As the tree chuckled softly, their jokes were fun.

Now each little critter has tales to tell,
Of the fruit that was funny, and danced so well.
Through gnarled branches, the laughter spilled,
A party of nature, all joy fulfilled.

Nectar in the Air

In a buzzing world where the flowers play,
Sweet nectar dripped in the sun's warm ray.
Bees wiggled and jiggled, so chubby and round,
Dancing like mad in the sweetest of sound.

A butterfly landed, a diva so bright,
"I'm here for the nectar, not here for a fight!"
The ants rolled their eyes with an exasperated sigh,
"Can't we just share? Oh my, oh my!"

The flowers were blushing, a riot of hues,
"Come feast at our banquet, we've got the best views!"
They twirled in the breeze, putting on quite the show,
While the bees formed a chorus - all buzzing in tow.

With nectar in the air and giggles all around,
The garden erupted in a joyous sound.
Nature's own comedy, a whimsical fair,
Where laughter grew wild, with nectar to share.

Pathways of Juice and Seed

Down the winding trail where the fruits do roll,
Little juice droplets were losing control.
"Careful!" cried the berry, "you're making a mess!"
"Let's race to the bottom, it's anyone's guess!"

With seeds like confetti, they splattered with cheer,
As they bounced off the pathway without any fear.
"Who knew being juicy could be so much fun?
Let's dribble and giggle till the day is done!"

An apple chimed in with a crisp little bite,
"Why rush, dear friends, when we can take flight?"
They plopped and they flopped, like a game of charades,
In the game of the orchard where laughter cascades.

Pathways of juice and seeds flying wide,
With laughter and play, they enjoyed the ride.
Each fruit had its part in the joyful parade,
In this jolly escapade where fun never fades.

The Odyssey of the Orchard

In an orchard so vast, where the sunlight spills,
Adventures unfolded on the sweetest hills.
A brave little kiwi with fuzz on its chin,
Said, "Join me, my friends, let the chaos begin!"

The lemons were laughing, all sour but spry,
While oranges rolled over, bursting with shy.
"Who knew we'd turn this into a play?"
The apples all chuckled, "Let's seize the day!"

A squirrel with acorns joined in the spree,
"My stash is your treasure, just follow me!"
They all marched together, what a curious scene,
With fruits and nuts forming a friendship routine.

The odyssey went through laughter and cheer,
With tales of the orchard spread far and near.
As sunset approached, they all felt so fine,
With memories to savor, all woven in rhyme.

Echoes of Orchard Lament

In the orchard where fruit does sway,
Bumbling bees hold grand ballet.
The apples giggle, the peaches tease,
While the pears plot mischief in the breeze.

A rogue wind blows, it sends them flying,
A pear hits Fred, and now he's crying.
With every bump, a joke they sing,
Oh! The laughter that fruit can bring!

When fruit bowl's full, it's clear to see,
A banana slips, oh woe is he!
The cherries chuckle, the lemons squawk,
A fruity fest, let's have a talk!

Underneath the leafy dome,
Fruits claim this orchard as their home.
In every shade and every hue,
There's silliness in all they do!

The Dance of Citrus Shadows

In a grove of zesty fun,
Lemons leap, oh what a run!
Tangerines roll with joyful glee,
Their citrus dance as wild as can be.

Grapefruits prance in polka dots,
Dancing 'round like silly knots.
They twirl and spin, and take a turn,
While oranges giggle and zestfully yearn.

A lime starts winking at a fig,
As wobbly fruits dance a jig.
Dancing shadows on the ground,
Echoing laughter, make it sound!

The sun sets low, the party's grand,
With fruity friends, oh isn't it planned?
In twilight's glow, they frolic free,
Zesty shadows, just wait and see!

A Voyage Through Orchard Trails

On a wagon made of rusty wood,
Riding through fruit, we've really should!
Pears chatter as they roll around,
Apples shout, 'Let's cover ground!'

A peach named Pete starts to sway,
'Hold on tight, I'm on my way!'
Through trails of berries, we make our mark,
Fruitful fun, from dawn till dark.

A grape brigade rolls down the lane,
Merrily singing in the pouring rain.
A melon's mischief, a slippery prank,
In this orchard, laughter's our rank!

With a chuckle and a cheerful shout,
We find ourselves, there's little doubt.
As we bounce and sway, we know it's true,
Every fruit's a friend, delightful and new!

Mysteries of the Bent Branch

Underneath the crooked tree,
Lies an old fruit, and come see!
A pear named Lou, with tales so tall,
Whispers laughter, one and all.

The oranges giggle, the apples ask why,
Lou grins wide as the tales fly high.
'Long ago, I danced with bees,'
Their buzzing laughter floats in the breeze!

The branches bend, they seem to sway,
Telling secrets of the day.
Every twist, a funny story,
In this grove of unexpected glory.

Mysteries unfold beneath the sun,
Every fruit here has had its fun!
And though the past is hard to catch,
It's a laughing feast, the perfect match!

www.ingramcontent.com/pod-product-compliance
Lightning Source LLC
Chambersburg PA
CBHW060134230426
43661CB00003B/418